A New True Book

SLEEPING AND DREAMING

By Rita Milios

Consultant: Dr. Edward Orecchio, Pediatric Neurologist
and Associate Director the Northwest Ohio Sleep
Disorders Center, Toledo, Ohio.

ℙ CHILDRENS PRESS ®

CHICAGO

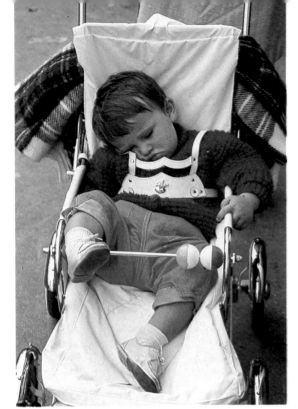

PHOTO CREDITS

AP/Wide World—25

© Cameramann International Ltd.—11 (top)

EKM-Nepenthe:
© Robert Eckert—Cover, 6 (bottom left)
© John Mahler—45 (top center)

Marilyn Gartman Agency:
© Norma Morrison—4 (top), 11 (bottom), 13 (right)

Courtesy Grass Instrument Company—17 (left)

Historical Pictures Service, Chicago—36 (2 photos), 37, 42, 44

Journalism Services:
© William DeKay—6 (bottom right)
© Richard Derk—31
© Joseph Jacobson—6 (top)
© Scott Wanner—45 (top left and bottom left)

Nawrocki Stock Photo:
© Robert Amft—23 (2 photos), 27, 38, 29
© Jeff Apoian—8
© David Bentley—4 (bottom), 32, 45 (top right and center)
Jim Wright—38

Courtesy The Ohio State University, Division of Sleep Medicine—14 (3 photos), 17 (right), 18 (2 photos), 19 (2 photos), 20, 34

Photri—2, 13 (left)

Tom Stack & Associates: © Tom Stack—45 (bottom right)
© Lynn Stone—30 (right)

Tom Dunnington—40, 41

Library of Congress Cataloging-in-Publication Data

Milios, Rita.
  Sleeping & dreaming.

  (A New true book)
  Includes index.
  Summary: A brief discussion of what we have learned about sleep and dreams from research.
    1. Sleep—Juvenile literature. 2. Dreams—Juvenile literature. [1. Sleep. 2. Dreams] I. Title.
II. Title: Sleeping and dreaming.
QP425.M55 1987   612'.821   87-14610
ISBN 0-516-01243-6

Childrens Press®, Chicago
Copyright ©1987 by Regensteiner Publishing Enterprises, Inc.
All rights reserved. Published simultaneously in Canada.
Printed in the United States of America.
1 2 3 4 5 6 7 8 9 10 R 96 95 94 93 92 91 90 89 88 87

TABLE OF CONTENTS

Sleep rests our bodies.

WHY DO WE SLEEP?

We all need sleep. Sleep rests our bodies. It allows time for our brains to do certain jobs, such as the making of memory records.

Some people seem to need more sleep than others do. Some healthy adults get by on three hours of sleep with no ill

Babies sleep about eighteen hours a day.
Older people do not need as much sleep.

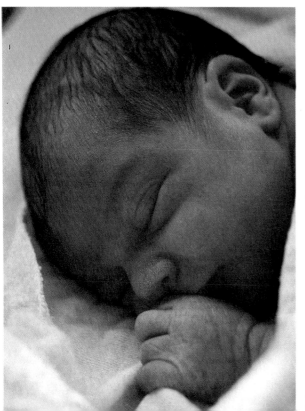

effects. Others feel tired if they sleep less than ten to twelve hours per night.

Babies sleep about eighteen hours a day. But by the time most people are ten years old, they have cut their sleep time to nine or ten hours per night. During their teenage years, most people have another drop in sleep time.

Teenagers sleep about eight hours.

A "normal" night's sleep
for a teenager is about
eight hours a night.

Every night when you go
to sleep, you enter a
strange and wonderful
world—the world of your
sleep and dreams.

WHAT HAPPENS WHEN WE SLEEP?

Even though you are not aware of it, your mind does not "turn off" when you sleep. Your brain continues to be active.

Scientists have recorded the sleep of adults. They have found that there is a pattern to this brain activity. This pattern or cycle repeats itself about every one and one-half hours, or about four to six times per night.

All night long, you are moving back and forth from a deeper sleep to a lighter sleep. You spend the most time in your deepest sleep stage during your first sleep cycle of the night. But as the cycles progress, you spend

Your brain never sleeps. It works while you sleep.

less and less time in deep
sleep. During the last
sleep cycle of the night,
you spend most of your
time in light sleep.

There are two main
types of sleep. REM and
NON-REM. Your REM
(rapid eye movement)
sleep is a lighter sleep
when your dreams occur.
During NON-REM sleep
your body rests and re-
energizes itself. People do
not remember the events

Not all sleeping is done at night or in bed.
Many people take naps during the day.

that occur during NON-
REM sleep.

During REM sleep, your
light sleep cycle, a strange
thing occurs. Many
physical changes take
place in your body. Your
pulse and respiration may
suddenly rise and fall.

13

FALLING ASLEEP

AWAKE	DROWSY	STAGE 1

RECTAL TEMP. CODE ➔

P.M. LEFT EYE ←
⎱ ELECTRO-OCULOGRAM
RIGHT EYE ←

ELECTRO-MYOGRAM (EMG)

LEFT CENTRAL EEG

RIGHT CENTRAL EEG

LEFT OCCIPITAL EEG — ALPHA RHYTHM DISAPPEARS

EKG

PROGRESSIVELY DEEPER SLEEP

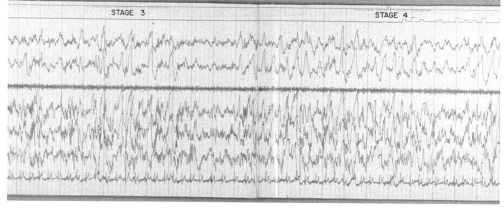

STAGE 3	STAGE 4

REM · DREAM · SLEEP

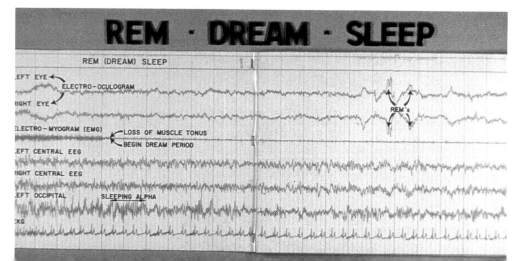

REM (DREAM) SLEEP

LEFT EYE ←
⎱ ELECTRO-OCULOGRAM
RIGHT EYE ←

ELECTRO-MYOGRAM (EMG) ← LOSS OF MUSCLE TONUS
← BEGIN DREAM PERIOD

REM's

LEFT CENTRAL EEG

RIGHT CENTRAL EEG

LEFT OCCIPITAL   SLEEPING ALPHA

EKG

Adrenal hormones like those produced during stress are secreted. Your eyes move in short, rapid, jerky movements. (For this reason, this sleep is called rapid eye movement, or REM, sleep.)

It is in the periods of REM sleep that your dreams occur. Since much of your final sleep time is REM sleep, you may wake up and remember a dream.

Opposite page: Graphs record brain wave activity during different periods of sleep.

SLEEP RESEARCH

In 1929, while studying brain activity, a scientist named Hans Berger at the University of Jena in Germany made an important discovery. He discovered that our brains produce constant electrical activity. He found out that this activity varies when

Hans Berger (left) discovered that the brain's electrical activity could be measured by an electroencephalograph, EEG, machine (right).

we are waking, sleeping, or involved in activity. To measure this electrical activity and its changes, Dr. Berger used a machine called an electroencephalograph, or EEG.

An EEG machine has wires attached to metal

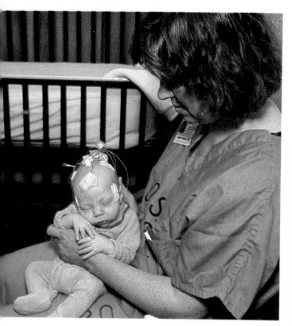

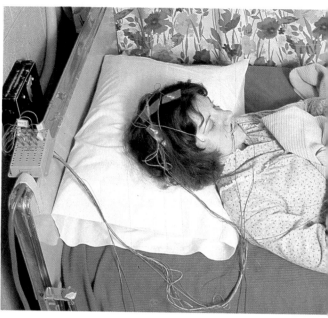

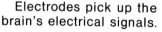
Electrodes pick up the
brain's electrical signals.

discs, called electrodes.
When these electrodes
were attached to a
person's body, the
electrical energy of a
person's brain could be
picked up. This electrical
activity could be amplified,

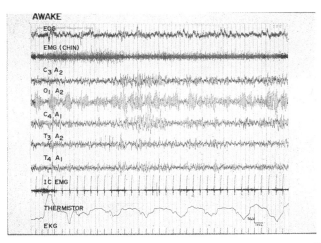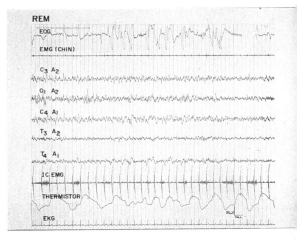

Brain waves made when the person was
awake (left) and during REM sleep (right).

or strengthened, in order
to produce signals. These
signals could then be
easily measured.

These electrical signals
were recorded on paper.
They made up and down
spikes or waves. These
"brain waves" varied in
height and width. It

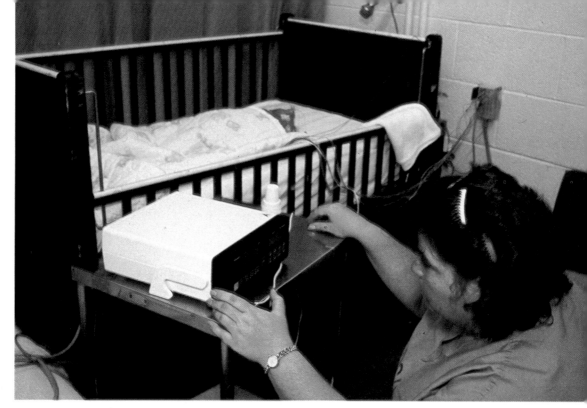

Nurse hooks up an EEG machine in order to measure brain waves.

depended on how relaxed or excited the person was during testing. Scientists still use the EEG machine to find out about abnormal sleep patterns and other problems.

WHY DO WE DREAM?

Some people think that they do not dream. But scientists tell us that we all have dreams during our REM sleep. Some people just don't remember their dreams.

Remembering a dream can be helpful. Sometimes in a dream we recall things we may have forgotten during the day. Dreams help our brains

"process" the day's
information.

Other times, dreams give
us messages about
ourselves. These messages
come from our "inner
selves," often called our
subconscious mind. It is
called subconscious
because it works below
the level of our conscious,
or waking, awareness. Your
subconscious mind uses

When we sleep our subconscious minds send messages to our brains.

your dreams to give you information and ideas you may not have noticed during the day. It also tells you how you really feel about things.

23

SIGMUND FREUD AND DREAMS

In 1890 a famous doctor named Sigmund Freud wrote *The Interpretation of Dreams*. He had discovered a new way to help some of his patients. He asked them to talk about their dreams and try

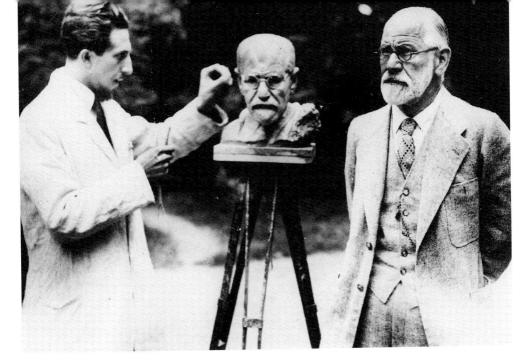

Sigmund Freud (right) posed for a sculptor in 1931.

to discover the message in their dreams. This process often helped the patients overcome their problems. Dr. Freud's method of working with patients became known as psychoanalysis.

STANDARD DREAM SYMBOLS

Your dreams contain your own special messages from your "inner self." But these messages do not come in words. They come in pictures. We each must "decode" our dream pictures, by noticing what feelings or attitudes these pictures bring out in us. But there are some dream symbols that seem

to mean the same thing to
many people.

You can start to decode
your dreams using these
"standard" interpretations.
Then try to understand
your personal symbols.
Remember that most

dream symbols will
represent a part of you—a
feeling, an attitude, a fear,
an idea.

A road or path often
represents your path in
life.

A house often represents
yourself—your mind or
body. The upper and lower

What does this
picture mean to you?
Do you think the
people are lonely?
Are they happy?

If you dreamed about this jumble of signs and symbols it could mean that you are confused about what direction you are taking.

levels may represent your conscious and subconscious minds.

Methods of transportation, cars, trains, buses, or airplanes, often mean the direction you are heading in life. A train going to the right can mean that you are "on the right track."

Animals may have many
different meanings in dreams.

Small animals often
represent children.
Kings and queens often
represent parents.

Pets often represent
loyalty and trust.
Schools often represent
learning.

Dreams about school often represent learning.

HOW TO REMEMBER YOUR DREAMS

Here are some tips to help you remember your dreams.

1. Just before you fall asleep, tell yourself: I am going to have a

dream. I am going to remember my dream. I am going to understand my dream message.

2. In the morning when you wake up, don't jump right out of bed. Lie quietly for a few moments and see what thoughts come into your

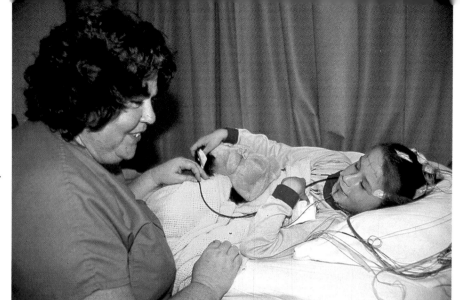

Children are used in sleep research studies.

mind. Often they will remind you of a dream.

3. As soon as you get up, write down your dream, or any parts of it that you can remember. Sometimes the forgotten parts of your dream will come to you later in the day.

CREATIVE DREAMS

People who create things—writers, musicians, scientists, inventors, or artists—often have ideas "pop" into their minds. Sometimes these thoughts come to people while they are awake. These ideas are called intuitions or inspirations. Other times they come in a dream—a creative dream.

Mozart (above) wrote operas and symphonies.
He said his music came to him in his dreams.

The famous composer,
Wolfgang Mozart, told
people that his music
came to him in dreams.
He created his
masterpieces by simply
writing down the notes to
the music he heard in his
dreams.

August Kekulé solved some of his problems in his dreams.

A dream helped a German chemist, August Kekulé, solve the long-time riddle of how a chemical was formed. In his dream he saw the chemical's parts, or molecules, as a snake with its tail in its mouth. He then solved the riddle, realizing that the

chemical's molecules were arranged in a ring.

You can have creative dreams, too. Try thinking about a plan, project, or problem just before you go to sleep. You may find that when you "sleep on it," an idea will come to you in a dream.

ODD SLEEP HABITS
AND MYTHS
ABOUT SLEEPING

Some people think they are awake when they are actually still sleeping. Sleepwalking is sometimes called somnambulism. It is more likely to happen to young children, but it does happen to adults, too.

A sleepwalker can walk
about the house and
around furniture unhurt.
Their subconscious mind
"sees," but their conscious
(waking) mind does not
remember what happens.

Sleepwalkers sometimes do funny things. Once a lady in England awoke to find that her sleepwalking butler had set a table for fourteen upon her bed!

Benjamin
Franklin

    Some people had
strange beliefs about
sleep. Benjamin Franklin
felt that cool skin was
important to a good night's
sleep. He slept with the
windows open, even in
freezing weather. He even
suggested everybody

should have two beds. When one bed got warm, the person could move to the cool bed!

Thomas Edison thought that sleep was a waste of time and a mark of stupidity. He claimed he slept only about two hours a night. In fact, he slept about four hours per night. He also took many short

Thomas Edison

naps during the day. Today we know that the time he spent during these naps was a time of great creativity. Perhaps we owe the light bulb to one of Edison's catnaps!

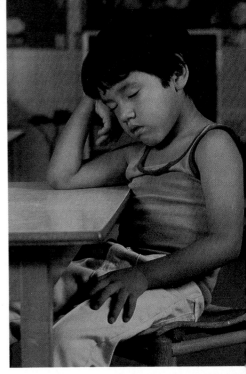
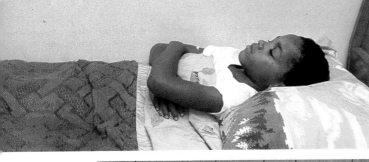
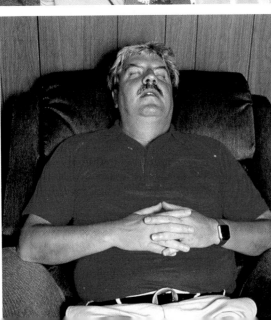
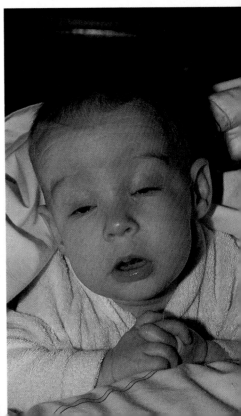

WORDS YOU SHOULD KNOW

abnormal(ab • NOR • mil) — unusual; different from the average

amplify(AM • pli • fy) — make larger, expand

attitude(AT • ih • tood) — a feeling or opinion about a person or thing

aware(uh • WAIR) — alert, alive, watchful

catnap(KAT • nap) — very short light nap

conscious(KON • shuss) — aware that one is alive; awake

decode(dih • KOHDE) — to change a coded message into ordinary language

detect(dih • TEKT) — discover, find out, uncover

energize(EN • er • jize) — make active; put energy into

hormones(HOR • moanz) — a substance formed by one organ and carried to another in a bodily fluid, causing it to function through chemical changes

inspiration(in • sper • RAY • shun) — an idea or action arrived at through some guiding influence

interpretation(in • ter • prih • TAY • shun) — explanation, translation

intuition(in • too • ISH • un) — knowing a fact without having used any reasoning ability

masterpiece(MASS • ter • peece) — the most excellent work of a skilled craftsman, musician, artist

molecule(MAHL • ih • kyool) — the smallest part, a tiny bit

non-REM — non-Rapid Eye Movement; sleep during which the body rests, without dreaming

process(PRAH • sess) — a system of actions, changes, or record-taking to arrive at an end

pulse(PUHLSE) — the regular throbbing of the arteries produced by heart beats

REM—Rapid Eye Movement sleep, the light sleep cycle, when
   dreams occur

secretion(sih • KREE • shun)—substance released by a bodily
   organ

subconscious(sub • KAHN • shus)—not totally conscious, but
   able to be made conscious

symbol(SIM • bul)—a mark, sign, emblem that represents the real
   object

INDEX

About the Author

Rita Milios lives in Toledo, Ohio with her husband and two grade-school children. She is a freelance writer and instructor in the Continuing Education department at Toledo University. She has published numerous articles in magazines including McCall's, Lady's Circle, *and* The Writer. *She is currently working on her first adult book. Mrs. Milios is the author of* I Am *in the Rookie Reader series and* Sleeping and Dreaming *in the New True Book series.*